The Nameless Sight

THE

NAMELESS

SIGHT

Poems 1937-1956

By Alan Swallow

Swallow Paperbooks

*

Acknowledgment is made to *American Poet, American Prefaces, The Bard, Calendar: 1942, College Verse, Colorado Quarterly, Crescendo, Experiment, Maryland Quarterly, The New Mexico Quarterly Review, The Old Line, Pacific, Palisade, Poetry: A Magazine of Verse, Prairie Schooner, Rocky Mountain Review, Signets, Talisman,* and *University of Kansas City Review* for permission to reprint here poems which first appeared in the pages of those magazines.

Many of the poems which are here reprinted from my three former collections have been revised extensively. For critical comments upon certain of these poems I am indebted to several persons, particularly to J. V. Cunningham, Robert Penn Warren, and Yvor Winters. I hope that they and others will approve any revisions which have been made.   A. S.

Books by Alan Swallow:

XI Poems · The Practice of Poetry · The Remembered Land
The War Poems · The Beginning Writer
The Nameless Sight: Poems 1937-56
An Editor's Essays of Two Decades

EDITOR: *Three Young Poets · Three Lyric Poets*
American Writing: 1942 · American Writing: 1943 · American Writing: 1944 (with Helen Ferguson Caukin) · Anchor in the Sea: An Anthology of Psychological Fiction · New Signatures 1948
Some Poems of Sir Thomas Wyatt · The Rinehart Book of Verse
Anthology for Basic Communication (with Iris Pavey Gilmore and Marion Huxoll Talmadge)
The Brand Book of the Denver Westerners, 1955

Contents

THE REMEMBERED LAND

Stone 11

Wyoming 1-6 12

Road South: Wyoming to Louisiana . . . 16

Journey 1-3 17

Landscape 19

Southern Landscape 20

Return to the West 21

Ghost Town: Night 22

The Cliff Ruin 1-2 23

THE REMEMBERED PEOPLE

To D. and H. 27

Letter to My Father and Mother 28

On the Gravestone of a Friend 29

The Word 30

For My Students 31

A Note 32

Return Flight from Missoula 33

NIGHT SONGS

Night Songs: for Mae 1-9 37

Praise for One 40

WAR POEMS

Year's End 43

Ode to Russia, 1943 44

For Mae 45

On the Outgoing Train 1-2 46

Communique from San Francisco . . . 47

Series for My Friends 1-5 48

"THE TOO MUCH LOVED EARTH"

Moment in November 55

Fog 56

Song in Ballad Measure 57

"The Too Much Loved Earth" 1-6 . . . 58

THE NAMELESS SIGHT

Poem 63

Closing the Year 64

The Watchman in *Agamemnon* . . . 65

State of Adolescence 66

The Field 67

The Skylight 68

Four Notes on Love 69

Poem 70

TWO POEMS FOR MY DAUGHTER

For My Infant Daughter 73

For My Daughter, Aged Five . . . 74

The Remembered Land

Stone

THE OLDER poets were wrong, speaking the lone
Imperturbable, imperishable, imponderable stone
Because a rock faced sun surviving human eyes.
For even stone dissolves and dies.
With wear of water, split of frost,
Stones break, and down the river-sewers are lost.

And feeble too those men who placed
A stone at the grave's end, now with the words effaced.

Who knows the hawk speaks well of rock and cliff,
Finding a haven there when wings are stiff.
And man in his hawk-days breathed life in stone,
Chipping and grinding it down, extending his bone.
Turn hammer words on rock, the fugitive:
So stone will live.

Wyoming

1. LOVERLESS she lies, an aging hag.
   What April wins is ill begot—
   In June the bastard leaves will sag.
   The lips of rain are soon forgot.

   Her breasts are clothed in fervid silk
   Of snow, and blizzards paw their slope.
   The nipples drip a bestial milk
   For mouths of deer and antelope.

   No man has thrust a plowshare point
   Into her smoothly flowing thighs
   But reaped a startled thing, disjoint
   With thirst, thirst haunting all its cries.

   Open she lies. Let any man
   Take her. And he will learn whereof
   Desire won death, and life began,
   The slim affair of love.

2. The coyotes raise the hood of light,
   Inviting darkness with their cries.
   It is the prairie dusk, and night
   Wavers, then boldly takes the skies.

   And falling on the hills, the dark
   Deepens the purple cloth to black.
   At last there is no agile mark
   Of hills for stiffened cardiac.

The stars elude the groping fingers:
The sun has taken all we tasted.
Here in the consciousness that lingers
The coyotes' hunger is not wasted.

3. Here on this cliff I've topped, my shadow blotting
   The edge of stone, the edge of flowing air,
   I watch the hawk assuming sky and plotting
   Unpenciled arcs on clouds' ascending stair.

   One step, and I'd go preying down to death,
   Swooping the towering altitudes I've stood,
   Folding my wings complacently as breath
   To take with my own beak my only blood.

   It is from blood I've climbed. The heart's slim trickle
   Has coursed the thoroughfare too long for rest.
   And even as I stand, time's early sickle
   Gathers the orange grain along the west.

   I will remember hawks find sleep on stone.
   This is a place to leave a silenced bone.

4. I cannot number all the pairs of feet
   That climbed this hill: many were moccasined,
   And some were clad in boots; and some were fleet,
   Some slow, some stiff against the pelting wind.
   And why should they attain this rising place?
   Perhaps to watch the hawk wing-folding sky,

Or take the warrior's privilege, to trace
His tenancy of sage and alkali.

They left no sign, no rock expressly turned.
The ground is smooth with wind and dust and rain,
The grass has often towered, leaned, and burned,
Leaving no single trace. *But never again*
Will the earth be quite the same, for after plow
This hill will wear a newly furrowed brow.

5. Here on this hill I take the coyote stance,
   Alert to trace mice-movement in the sage
   And stiff, defeated grass. With hovering glance
   I read this watermarked old parchment page.

   And it is old. It's old with frosted rot.
   The slanting light of southward moving sun
   Displays a ragged edge, thumb-smear, a blot,
   And faded lines where eyes have quickly run.

   There is no movement now. The tale is reaped,
   And marketed, and stalks no more. Tonight
   Let snow erase it, cold and blizzard-heaped.
   There will be other tales to write.

6. In this almost forgotten valley I
   Have stood alone beneath the mountain rim,
   Soil under foot, and blanketed by sky,
   And watched the western fires turn red and dim;
   The light *which suffers blindness* leaves the air

To cold, and to the world-wind's throated sally;
The mountains flatten, are no longer there;
And I am in the universal valley.

O world, I want to etch upon my brain
The unhorizoned earth, the earth that any star
Can know! *It's cold.* And there is war in Spain.
Now bed, and sleep, and hear the wind's catarrh.
Some morning I hope to wake, look up with eyes
Content, and find this valley paradise.

Road South: Wyoming to Louisiana

RAPACIOUS moss obscures the sky,
Makes trees go crouching ways:
The earth is stirred with green awry,
And no wind ever drives the days.

We have come South from sterile hills
That lift a callow breast in air,
That breed what color man distils
With water, plow, and stubborn care.

To travel South is not to take
A road, but rapid skier's slide:
Down altitudes of air we break
To land that opens level, wide.

And now we lie in shade and drink
The ready ozone, do not dare
To probe what soil is under, or think
Of hunting heights we once could bear.

Journey

1. LEAVING the pines, the livid canyon,
   The car picks speed, takes perilous poise
   On top the wide and rolling waste,
   The steering troubled by wind's threat and noise;

   The daylight burns aloft, and spreads
   The fire within the barren wood
   And wields, like hammer rapping steel,
   The temper of the ancient blood.

   On silence, in a silent land,
   Narrow the slitted, scouting eye;
   The sights will harden in the hand
   And kick one puff of alkali.

2. Coasting the rolling Middle West,
   The flushed hills curving down into
   The fleshly cup, the stream's slow pool
   Which shapes in sand large heaven's blue;

   Roots grip the hillsides, lie more warm
   And fertile in the bottoms, a sea
   Of floating green where insects swarm
   Beneath the sun's quick treachery.

3. The last rock south along the river
   Lifts its vernal covering;
   Beyond, earth's sediment lies level
   Beneath the buzzard's hovering;

   The great winged shadows ride
   Such bearded trees; deep in their shade
   Wing's flickering hardly touches
   The sea where casual eyeballs wade;

   And, submarine, the quiet air
   Is ready to the tasteless tongue,
   The beast sits in it overhead,
   And breath lies heavy in the lung.

Landscape

THE SEDIMENTARY world, unfolded, heavy
With sleep, feeds on dropped needles from the mountain
    pine
And sand wind-worried from the mountain stone,
Deposits where the rivers roll and shine.

(I wonder if this geological note
Has meaning: All ages are old beyond
Eyes that on green savannahs paused and paced;
But drowned long since in some widening pond.)

Magnolias weight the air with bloom. The oak,
Gathering green leaves and faded moss, has need
Of rot. The leaf's green flesh is high within
The vulture's tent, and where the vultures feed.

And in this vernal world the man must eye
The long-beaked birds riding their silent blade.
The end adds sediment. And it is easy
To fuel mind's splintered flame within green shade.

Southern Landscape

UNDER magnolias now the air
Weighs heavy on the lovers' arms:
The dreams that lay in love's long stare
Are spoiled by harms.

Without the woven shade, flashes
The heated earth, the burning sun:
Within, the dark analysis
Of love is done—

Uneasy love is forged. The two
Lie back with thunder in the ear
And, as the world turns over new,
Step out with fear.

Return to the West

THE ROCKIES rise, unforgettable and alone:
How bare the sawteeth stand in eastern light!

If old Jim Bridger lies uneasy, Custer
With the golden hair, it is a pity. The earth
Has had them long enough, and those who plundered
In violence of pride, to know their worth.

Now as the day and night return the silt
Of time, and now return the wanderers—
If these in pines renounce their former guilt,
Even the prodigal the earth endures.

Ghost Town: Night

WHAT TIME has left, now falls in night.
Our blanket lies between decay
And fire: wood, stone are crumbling: late
We felt the flanks of youth delay,

Warmed with the crimson flush of blood,
Warmed with the violent sunset air.
Long since, blood thickened on the spade
Which rang on stone already bare.

Rock ridge and saddle—these have held
The blows of valiant men—this is the place
They slept, whored, slobbered in the mould,
And stared upon death's casual face.

We turn us toward night's sleep—to dream,
To shudder in that fondest praise—
To wake in sunlight, lured and warm,
And helpless in that ignorant maze.

The Cliff Ruin
An essay in archaeology

1. WHERE is the dream? In dust I stand
   Where once stood many others;
On wells of dust I place my hand
   (Power of dust will make us brothers,

   Whose strength for guileless centuries ran
      Through unshackled brain and bone),
   Where now I stand once stood a man
      On whom the sunlight shone,

   And shone with that incessant play
      Which ripens everything,
   Even its favorite, to decay
      And powders the bird's wing.

   Where is the dream? It never held
      But shadow of the sky
   And with that darkness moved compelled
      To look with sightless eye.

2. Here by this ancient, foundering wall
      I find a shard of clay
   Once glazed in fiery ritual
      Against its crumbling away.

Yet here it lies, a fragment only
    Of work in earth and fire.
What shape was meant, austere and lonely,
    Is one I should admire

If I might see where pride once shown,
    And hold in the still mind,
In its view over the hard, waste stone,
    That dream death would unwind.

The Remembered People

To D. and H.

I SEE YOU stand in snow. I see the snow,
In blizzard driven, run the gullies, speed
Over the town with thresher knives; and stayed
By you, standing; by house and fence and weed.

The drifts you gather stay when you are gone,
A shadow more imperishably formed
By wind and winter weather than by sun:
Destroyed by shovel, or by April warmed.

This is our day, this day the blizzard blunders:
And though we find no charity to give,
Or wander south to hear the rainstorm thunders,
We are not wasting, but in winter live.

Letter to My Father and Mother

WHEN LAST we talked, last year's manure had found
The shriveled roots and greened the stricken grass.
And we were animated, gesturing
Automatons whose day, whose year, would pass.

We spoke of parting. Words like water spread.
The grass would need more water on the morrow.
But in the hour allotted out of Time
One gesture, only a word, suffices sorrow.

Now I have seen banana leaves shredded
With wind, the sagging shreds brittled by frost.
Here in the South the easy foliage blankets
The earth, gives easy fruit, is easily lost.

Though we seek winter refuge, the calendar sun
Denies us hibernation from deceit.
For where in promise is the act undone?
And where in spring frost's nimble cheat?

On the Gravestone of a Friend

STRANGE monument! on which the words will fade,
Ever be nameless as is he within the shade.
He lies with darkness in his dreamless head
And has no use for words we once had said—
Nor for his laughter, his rough body's speed.
Needless he lies, and cannot know my need.

The Word

for a writers' workshop in the Rockies

THESE FACES warm and smile, but laughter lies
Uneasy in the throat. For what can be
More serious than incubus of pen?
Here brims the sun, water, the mountain tree—

But how indifferent, how marvelous!
There moves one hand we cannot know or tell.
And we are serious—visited by words
Whose quarrel drives the brain within its shell.

Grandeur is not ours, indeed. It lies
Upon that slope where water finds the lichen.
When we forget our dreamed idolatries
The ironical word shall find us fit, less stricken.

For My Students

WHAT IS unnamed, we heal.
What is unopened, tear and close.
    What is unclean,
We suffer, and experiment with hope.

    What is within, discover;
What is without, bring warm to home.
    Whatever seems in wonder,
We hold, and give it shape of hope.

A Note

WHAT BITTERNESS assails the ravaged mind,
And disappointed spectres were my friends,
Ah ghosts, sleep well; from slumber wake to find
That love is faithful, love will make amends.

Return Flight from Missoula

BIG HORNS, Big Horns. I fly the mighty wave
Diminished as the day diminishes;
The sky bends one day toward the grave.

                                        This day
I said good-bye to Bitter Roots; I guess
What thought has changed the heart, and in what way.

Walter, I think there's gold dust on your trail,
Or some black-banded ore your gentle pace
Discovers veined within the rock.

                                        I talk
To wish sun-warmth upon the mountain shale,
Sun-warmth forever on your face.

Macky, neither wisdom nor virtue "may requite
The shifting and the many-shaded."

                                        One
Remembers beauty long after it is faded,
Resolves to cherish all the heart of night
And hold all locked into oblivion.

Night Songs

Night Songs: for Mae

1. THE WORLD has age tonight. The fires of stars
   Are dim as embers found in midnight pine,
   Red eyes inflamed against the falling dark.
   This crumbling, spun-out world is yours and mine.

   Under the long-stemmed pine we lay with love;
   Or watched dark shadow move upon the stone—
   Unhesitant it moved, and fell in time
   Shapeless across your warm and shapely bone;

   Or as the night, the gaping mouth, hunted
   The mountain, harried us in the caverned trees—
   Aroused, we kept the loping feet at bay,
   Lighting a space with our small secrecies.

   And now as darkness builds toward dawn, there is
   No quiet. Night towers once, moves restlessly,
   Leans in the west. And we shall wake to find
   The horizon's stealth, far as we can see.

2. THE GREAT TREE held its summer over us,
   The bole, the inner leaves, still warm with blood;
   But slowly, frost dropped leaf by leaf, to wither
   That aging sap in its ambitious flood.

   We saw a hawk poised for an hour aloft;
   But who could tell—his bladed wings were still—
   What searching eyes had seen the rabbit soft
   And bundled, ready for the instant kill?

So we regarded time this hour: we knew
The season changed, frost's ice upon the land,
While sap within the shrinking tubes withdrew
And your warm body cold beneath my hand.

Aubade

3. AROUSED, the body turns, becomes aware:
    That head creasing the pillow is one I know
    At evening taut with worry and with care,
    But now like latticed branches calmed with snow.

    The dreams I wake from ghost the morning flower,
    No stranger to the day's own kind of deceiving;
    Before this life, or death, there is this hour
    To look on beauty troubled with sleep, by its breathing.

    Sunlight nudges the windowsill, perfect
    And calm, spills over, spreads along the floor;
    The room awakes from dream, becomes object
    Shapely and real to eyes: bed, chair, and door—

    How long have I known these? Not long in Time,
    A quiet stone in what immeasurable sea.

    Now men put off identity of home
    And night; we wake to time for you and me.

4. IT IS ENOUGH that we can turn alone
    Into the world and see the sun on stone.
    It is enough that we can see the night
    Come down, and do not feel the need of light.

5. NIGHT closes the eye upon the world we know.
    But the wise eye sees your flesh upon the night.
    Ah fond dream! There you cannot turn and go.
    Without that eye I have no need of sight.

6. THE SNOW sags on the eaves:
    Cold leans upon the door:
    The wind unwinds and leaves
    Desire crouching on the floor.

7. I HAVE LIVED much at night—where self will move
    In insecurity and security of love,
    The dark expand and hear the power surge
    Within the image of her who can be love.

8. THE BIRDS of myth, with giant wing,
    Plunder the night with ancient fire:
    From dreams I wake with their desire,
    Their gentleness, their suffering.

9. AND WHEN I wake from dream, the stars have
            known you,
        For they have ridden the lonely night;
    Great universe of love they have bestown you.
        Ah, dear one in their nameless sight,
        May I rise gladly to your light.

Praise for One

IT WAS your birthday; and we who had been wed
Had mentioned age, trying to see in time's
Unmurmuring channel where the channel led.

Firm in repose, the lamplight swept your face.
The darkness was at home. And in your eyes
Smouldered that look which love had made more wise.

War Poems

Year's End

THAT YEAR the Caucasus was cold
  And guns disturbed the snow;
The ancient witted slavs were bold
  And the warm blood would flow.

And winter glazed Himalayan air
  Where, over stone, the planes
Fed solace to the Asian fare,
  Went homeward to those veins.

And in the Pyrenees have stood
  Poor refugees from love
Who each within the iron wood
  Goes down to a separate cove.

Ode to Russia, 1943

REMEMBER the golden wheat, remember the field
Where daisies stood, where sheep moved low in clover:
In richness boys have played, and men have stood
With shadowed eyes to watch the rain come over.

But there the field was red with blood, with blood.
The bodies lie in gesturing attitudes.
The bodies lie, and quietly unbud.
Anxious they lived their living platitudes.

What hand placed the rifle? The hand of fear
Has touched some trigger on our history;
And death may sit and meditate its food,
Lecherous, vain in its ignorant piracy.

The Soviet airman eyes the fields of dead.
Anger shall fix the sight of gun, shall pull
The tendon in the wrist: anger see red
Spot with vengeance no gesture will annul.

So who will lie him down, careless in sleep?
Anger and justice will meet that brutal shock:
Causes for valor some have learned to keep
And not those causes, guardless, let unlock.

For Mae

EACH NIGHT in public stations
Sit those more lonely than the homeless;
And, rising to embrace,
Kiss frightened lips
And inadvertent tears.

And thus were we. I rose
To follow, follow after—
To think: at eight o'clock
She left Denver, at twelve,
Cheyenne.

        What are those places,
Those towns we shuttle through?
They are not ever known
Except as names where I
Would touch your reaching hand.

On the Outgoing Train

1. THOSE little settlements—
   Sediments of outrageous time
   Upon the dark north tundra—

   Echo the voice of trains
   Which chatter their iron wheels
   Over the worn face of the land.

   What have we left behind?
   Some harvest we meant to share
   In the sworn fiesta of home.

   Those sober houses, clustered
   But separate, sit quietly the plain
   Formal as the stone hand of love.

2. YOU FADE down many tracks—
   On many roads I follow you.
   In Russia, China, Yugoslavia,
   Those foreign, yet familiar, faces
   Turn like kind and sober brothers
   To share our loneliness.

                    Dear Love,
   Within their hope we find our home:
   We share their struggle and their fame;
   In all their lands you comfort them,
   In all their names they speak your name.

Communique from San Francisco
June, 1945

DEAR SIR:

Who is the one provoked
To poetry within our time?
The war has guns and words, and needs
The speaking guns; through war we climb
Like senators in politics—
Vague in the vast pantomime.
And those who wake up with the dead
Daily unlearn the old sublime.

How does one know a history
Of those who make it unaware?
Somewhere among them lies a hope
Which hangs its tired, ironical dare
In the heads of all, and moves their blood.
Now on the San Francisco air
High fog covers the conference,
A history, and a slugging war.

Series for My Friends
Honorable Discharge, AUS, November, 1945

1. SOMETHING about a cause has put us deep,
   Something we once defined, but do not know
   If anyone's words have caught our own. The sleep
   Of those who fell upon Caucasian snow,
   Of those whose blood re-wet the soil of France
   Or harried Japs from names which fell like stars
   From the vast eye of the East—sleep stilled that chance,
   And various men have wept those various wars.

   Would we be minister to history,
   Present some word in the international brief?
   Yes, once were we prepared, and might yet be
   The envoys of an empty shell of grief
   And wordless stand in wordless centuries,
   Stiff and ungainly in our prophecies.

2. THIS HERITAGE was great: the fields of grain,
   Or sugar beets in watered rows; gaunt towns
   Which spread their secret need on hungry plain
   Or followed huddled in the mountain shade.
   Children, we little knew this need, nor knew
   That in a hidden impetus we played—
   Careless of frenzy, we dropped our clothes to plunge
   The running water; in flushing birds would shout
   And loose our gunfire on the silent hills.
   The heritage was brief, a home we lost,

Foreclosed of all but sunlight on the sills;
The lengthening bones which took us to the fen—
There, to that suffering wilderness, we came
With innocence and appetite of men.

3. WHAT HAD the vision held? Justice, perhaps,
And care of brother and brother; the simple hand
Outstretched, but not in charity or greed;
Symbols of man a stone, water, man's speech,
White motion of the oar. Thus small again,
A man might live his land, a simple swain.

Visions are always with us; where we move
We never reach, as if we were not for love.

4. WHAT SHALL we say for those who lost,
In many lands many a brother?
They settle meekly under frost,
And like dead leaves cover each other.

Salute with guns, or speak each name,
Lost fathers of their victories—
Ready to leave his blood each came
To coral sands and coral seas?

The winds of honor touch their graves.
They peaceful lie in honorable waiting
Who dot the islands no one saves.
The soldier's anger is abating.

5. AND SO one turns, returns, the echo
   Of former platitudes. What say
   The men of word, ambassadors
   Of plenty in the narrow line?

   Dark Eliot mourns beyond the sea
   And Pound becomes a beggarman.
   Red Warren knows, vast Red in shadow,
   That love will shake a wizened hand;
   And Tate wants beer with wine.

   Grave Winters fills a mighty head,
   Slandered by those unknown to worth,
   That javelin. Young Cunningham's
   Green wit is growing warm.

   How many admiration names!
   Stevens, whose head is rich and snug;
   And Carlos Williams, alter ego;
   Van Doren, Ransom, Auden, Frost.
   And Hardy, Robinson, old Yeats,
   And spoiling Crane among those dead
   Who speak our language yet.

   Or more, the twenty younger men
   And women, whose work is sheaf or book.
   And I, who read and printed words,
   Work warm within that marvelous air.

Return? The soldier turns to home
To find it moved; and walks, like poets,
Unguarded through the trees.

*"The Too Much
Loved Earth"*

Moment in November

HERE ON our eyes
The senile fabric of summer lies.

What in this moment has the pulse detected?
What, the rapid heart, the flowering blood, expected—

The thinnest month, the rivers thin,
Snow blowing down, frost creeping in?

Fog

THE MIST has washed upon us
  Beneath the oak,
Deepening the gloom of heaven
  And its dark cloak.

A grayish place we have
  Of fog and leaves,
Quiet of joy and laughter,
  Quiet of eaves.

We watch the gloom, sit backs
  Against the bole,
And know in time's loosening
  Little to control.

Song in Ballad Measure

AT HARLOWTOWN the cattle feed,
    At Buffalo the sheep:
And why should we, who have such need,
    Time's alien shadow keep?

At Baton Rouge the river rolls,
    At Yellowstone it leaps:
The channeled stream of night controls
    Mock lips that silence keeps.

Wind in the Kansas wheat is flooding,
    Rain moves the mountain pine:
And in one's head the chimes are brooding
    Their hourly valentine.

The Rio Grande carries silt,
    The hills are aged to clay:
And we who have so soberly built
    Defend what falls away.

"The Too Much Loved Earth"

1. THE RED LEAF smoulders in its grave.
   Uphill, the gaunt pines blacken, die
   Their rigid deaths, with overhead
   The innocent and startling sky.

   The bronze earth turns and changes face.
   One season builds its vernal tide.
   What ancient wash, what flameless fire
   Is this that holds the mountainside?

2. THE EAVES stop the sunlight from the wall,
   Where termites thrust their whispering jaws, and mice
   Run channels of desire. Within, will fall
   The chortling finger, and the lips' advice.

   At last into their dust the termites slip,
   The mice falter in lust's own stratagem,
   The smile and word shall perish on the lip;
   And the kindly wall shall cover them.

   Epitaph for One Who Burned Both Ends
3. LOVER OF WARM and shallow deeps,
   Earth mothered him within her womb.
   And now that he is spent, he sleeps
   Contented in the fleshless tomb.

4. INSATIATE AUTUMN, sap is last: it draws
   In shrinking tubes of ice its close belief
   And as the rodent tooth of winter gnaws
   Dreams on the fragile limb, the fragile leaf.

5. LET VIOLENCE be!
   Let loose the groping hand!
   It's much to know that we,
   The dying, walk this land.

   Autumn
6. I HEARD his ruined breath
   Crack in the barley sheaf
   And salvaged from the realm of death
   A single, and yellowed, leaf.

The Nameless Sight

Poem

CALM SEA of time is on us, and we move
Toward the fact of our lives. Which way in time
Lie the lost faces—small, hard, and fleshless faces?
Present and innocent, and lost in time,
We are held, awash, from death's stately places.

The past is not the past, content, unchanging,
But feeds upon this present hour, which hies
Us toward some shore—fringed, one might believe,
With calm sand and the green grass. What lies
Unburied is we who move without our leave.

Closing the Year

TIME MOVES to impale the closing year.
The season's wound has bled, and it will heal:
Rocks crumble, and the grasses sere
Under the ruin of the aged and ageless wheel.

Here in the northland seed has run
Like snow among the hills, threaded like mice
The stubble passageways, and lain
Like living beetle in momentary ice.

What can be buried? Even the husk
Rots, and then finds the vein: and over all
Time spills its moving seas, whose rush
Leaves no locked island of decent burial.

The Watchman in Agamemnon

TWELVE MONTHS the blank sea stared, and worked
    unmoved
Beneath his lidless eyes:
                    and overhead
The gulls screamed, and the stars poured handsome light;
Nor warmth, nor cheer, nor stone for bed.

Turned in on his night, his eyes were unafraid,
Knowing the crumbling walls, the victor's wrath,
The sea bloody; and saw at last the fire
Still to be fed by death's own stinking breath.

State of Adolescence

"A world where bunnies ripened in the sun."—Gladys Hyde

DEAR IDIOT, who loves his goodly teacher,
Kisses her mouth on a cold and moonlit road,
Or fumbles toward the vague, inviting loin,
Whose dog kicks fleas forever like a goad,

What would you learn? Great rafters of the night
Contain your arrogance, contain your chase
Like pastures where the vagrant pollen stands
And guttural bees turn home from the golden race.

Put off this dream—or touch the impertinent breast
And clasp the mistress of the ivory horn
Which nuzzles shame. Witness your changeling there,
His ashes left forbidden and forlorn.

The Field

RABBITS push blunt noses to the leaf,
Secret mice find sprouts with silent jaws,
In air the hawk sits lordly as the thief,
Where robins mutter the bright crow caws.

Earth's deep minerals seethe and work, create
This green segment of eternity;
Grass leans with the wind upon the gate
Which will plunge with the leaf and the sterile bee.

Lord of such domain, man sees with pride
A leaf-machine store food against his drouth;
Knows in mind, or the heart's vulnerable side,
That he shall be the grass within the rabbit's mouth.

The Skylight

NIGHT: bed and blanket: through that pane
The stars. Poised for my contemplation
Far light pools cold upon the plane
And useless to the nation.

So does the glass control the light—
Contained, reflected, and let through—
A crystal shaped by my delight
For shaft, the stalking view.

Four Notes on Love

1. LOVE is experience—
   With your fine head of sense
   You bare that loneliness
   In which I stroll the corridor
   And learn but less and less.

2. LOVE is experience—
   That place we always lose
   But always gain with sense.
   Whatever flows is gone, but the flow.
   In me that flow delivers love.

3. EXPERIENCE is blind?
   But you, my love, would not be blind.
   Experience shall fashion nothing; it must move.
   I do not move except to fashion love.

4. LOVE is experience—
   The making of the flow to sense.
   And when we move from that drear hunger
   (In which the hand is moved like water)
   To will the hand to move,
   I would place my hand in sense
   Upon your hand in love.

Poem

ONCE, WHEN the mountain shoulders turned
   To gather rocky clusters in the skies,
The fire was speechless that we burned,
   Voiceless, our night sighs:

And speechless lay the hurrying night,
   Voiceless were the moment and the hour;
Vague breezes moved the feeble light;
   No thing had power.

Lazy were words within the mind
   And soft the words upon the lip; there, dumb,
Great strength grew in us, cold, to find
   The perishing womb.

Two Poems
For My Daughter

For My Infant Daughter

DEAR CHILD, child of the human night,
The starless beaming of our fear,
Error, ingratitude, and war—
Dear child, I grieve for your birthright
Beneath these heavens: see, this year,
How blind, how deep the wound and scar.

What shall I offer besides love
And gratitude? What counsel give
Upon a planet hot with blood?
May you grow wiser than the dove
Whose passion, warm but relative,
Sits like the leaf, and the leaf's bud.

May you grow beautiful with grace
Of limb and movement; may your mind
Grow fonder of the time's decease
Than of its habitual, easy place—
More than conservative, to find
That more than earthly blessing, peace.

I hope too much? Yes, hope for all
That state, my human child, which shone
In many eyes, when the world shook,
And is not dead but yet may fall
On you, dear woman worthy grown,
On me, grown worth your backward look.

For My Daughter, Aged Five

Toss your blond-red curls.
Touch the merry nose;
Where your eye unfurls
Time in promise goes
Joyous past the thornèd rose.

Where your eye unfurls
Promised hill and hollow
Time your path uncurls
Where I cannot follow,
Thornèd hill and thornèd hollow.